MW00896256

"A Made Over Woman Anthology"

I wish I knew

Copyright © 2020 by Taisha' Nichole the Brand

www.Taishanichole.com

All rights reserved. No part of this book may be reproduced or transmitted in any form or by any means without written permission from the author.

Holy Bible, New International Version®, NIV®

Copyright ©1973, 1978, 1984, 2011 by Biblical, Inc.®

Used by permission.

All rights reserved worldwide.

~Broken To Glow ~

We are All Glow Sticks
A Glow Stick can Only Serve its Purpose when it's Broken

-Taisha' Nichole

Purpose

The purpose of this anthology is to encourage, inspire, uplift and help women. These series of stories are things we wish we knew, things we've learned, how we've endured and have overcome the many obstacles in every different aspects of our lives. We pray that you gain hope, peace and understanding from our stories. Apply each story to your life so that you may avoid red flags and gain guidance through your own situation.

Table of Contents

Marriage

They Thought It was Over After the Boomerang

Subtitle: "It Didn't Work"

By Ondia Wyatt Petty

S everal years have gone by and I am walking in my purpose. I prayed for healing and wholeness in my life entirely. God definitely heard the prayers of the righteous. I have lived a life causing pain to a lot of others and I never thought about what I've done to others coming back on me, or even on my children.

God humbled me, softened my heart, allowed me to deal with those demons from my childhood so that I could be a better version of myself. People could not believe I was this new person. I prayed to God to make me into the wife he ordained me to because I was ready to get married. See I was married in 2003, but I was too young and didn't know who I was, let alone what being a wife was.

First, I had to understand two people will become one, all that INDEPENDENT stuff was out the door and being humble was a must. Second, I had to understand that I had to be able to support my husband. Meaning he's the head of the wife and Christ is head of the husband but the wife is the neck and husband is the head. So the wife helps hold up the husband. Boosting him up. Being his number one fan even when you feel like you have no one supporting you. Third, I had to respect my husband in private, public and especially in front of the children. One thing we must know is that disrespect is such an ugly trait and it will allow outsiders to not respect you or your spouse. Fourth, I had to learn to be discreet in my conversations, the way I dress, and how I carry myself when my husband is present and not present.

Fifth, I had to understand that inner beauty was more important than the outer beauty. I can't spend more time fixing up my hair, applying makeup, dressing in the best clothing if my attitude is nasty, I'm bitter, I'm angry, I'm resentful, evil, have malice in my heart, hold grudges and just down right dark on the inside. Eventually that what's on the inside runs to the outside, so if it's toxic it'll not only damage you but those around you.

Last, I had to understand that being his freak was a must. All that freaky stuff I did when I was single only matters with my husband. Therefore, do whatever you have to do to keep the bedroom booming!!

So here it is 2015 and I met a guy and we talked at first then stopped because it just wasn't the right timing for us. A few months went by and we met up again and I prayed to God, if this is the man for me, make it easy for me to love him and him to love me. We started to date and things began to fall in place, so we talked about a future together and goals. I mean this man was the best thing I've ever had. He spent time with the children without me having to ask. He respected my wishes to not have sex before marriage. Did I mention he was saved and loved the Lord just as I did? He stepped in as the head and that spoke volumes. This would be both of our second marriage and we promised God that this was not going to end the way our previous relationships ended.

We completed marriage counseling and got married April 22, 2016. That was one of the happiest days of my life. I even believe God gave me some extra anointing for stepping in alignment with his will! I was singing and operating my gifts under the power of God like never before. Things were going great and we had no complaints until we received a call that my husband's grandfather had died. I rushed home from work so that I could be there for my husband and family and keep him covered as a wife should.

During this time my husband became very mean, evil, vulnerable, and several gates or cracks were created in my marriage and the enemy was overly excited about trying to destroy what God had joined together. Previously, I did mention we weren't having any problems and never anything major but the little things like not spending time together, always on our cell phones, and things like that created major problems for us.

My husband is a full time musician and I assist him with singing, whether it be leading worship, teaching parts, or just filling in wherever I'm needed. God opened the door for my husband to take on a job as a Music Director at a church prior to his grandfather passing and we all know ladies love musicians. I mean I'm married to one so I definitely know. There was a young chick with a couple of children and she was not ugly and honestly she was the type my husband would like. I wasn't worried about her at that time because I thought we were good. I didn't realize how much my husband's grandfather's death had affected him, which caused a major wedge between us.

So this young, attractive, nicely put together chick would smile in my face, reach out to me for encouragement, I mentored her, she studied how I sang, how I dressed and even began to hold conversations with my husband at inappropriate times. Her children would speak to me but they would run and jump all over my husband as if they knew him on another level. I'd ask him about it and he would say "it's nothin' India, I'm the Minister of Music and they love me." I didn't pay much attention to it after he said that. Then the young chick and my husband's behavior changed towards me. She blocked me on Facebook but kept my husband as her friend. She would ask him for money and not a small amount of money either. I would ask her questions but she would have an attitude; like I don't understand why I have to explain anything to you. It took everything in my body to not knock the living daylights out of her. God was definitely my portion. If I asked my husband questions he would defend her and tell me I was just insecure.

One day she posted a picture on Facebook before she blocked me of a plate of food. Ironically it was my husband's favorite meal, boneless chicken breast, green beans with potatoes, and yellow rice. I made a joke about the picture not knowing the next day I'd see one of our good friends that told me they had just seen my husband the day before at the grocery store. I knew he wasn't buying our house food so I asked him if he saw what he bought and said yes it was some chicken, a can of green beans and something else. My heart dropped to my feet because I knew what was going on.

There were many situations that happened like her driving the Jeep that I co-signed for, her posting pictures of her in the Jeep, her telephone bill recurring on his bank account, him getting a hotel room with a jacuzzi, and the fact he was always in the area she lived in around her family. Mind you her whole family attended the church we attended. They knew what was going on and saw me week after week. Does any of this sound familiar? She and I almost got into a physical fight in the church because she bumped into me but she knew everyone would be on her side because I was on her territory. Even my husband defended her. Seems like this was me on the other side of the fence but 10 times worse.

You would think that would be all the evidence I needed but nope I stayed right there, fasting and praying. Asking God to give me clear evidence and answers. This girl had studied me so she knew what I said and did that would make him mad and she was doing all she could to make sure she got my husband.

One late night my husband was sleeping and I couldn't sleep for some reason and the Holy Spirit said check his phone, so I did and what did I find? A video of my husband and this chick having sex. The worst part about it was watching the way he rubbed her butt and touched on her on that video. I could feel the passion he had for just by seeing that and let me know he had some deep feelings for this chick. So I woke his butt up and showed him what I found. He says that's not her that's someone else.

First of all sir, you were hitting her from the back but she turned around so I saw her face. On top of that she had just posted a picture on the same day with the same dress on and same hairstyle. So explain that! He said well I used a condom but that's beside the point. He apologized and apologized and said he didn't talk to her anymore and he wasn't in his right mind so he had left her alone, but he forgot to delete the video. Oh yeah, no problem, I deleted it for you and the pictures she sent. I even called her and of course she hung up on me. I walked outside to pray because that's always my lifeline and the Lord spoke and said "Be still and do not move." I didn't understand why God would allow me to stay in a marriage where infidelity had taken place.

Time went on and we were working through this mess but I was traumatized to the point I would replay them having sex while we were having sex. It was hard for me and every woman I saw would remind me of her and that situation. I had to really seek some counseling to get over this situation. My trust was gone so I thought, so God reminded me one day of who and what I used to do.

See there were times when I wasn't in my right mind and I did things I'm not proud of and God with his merciful, forgiving self spared me. He also replayed the time in my life where I was the side chick to the married man. He said the way you are feeling, is the same way that man's wife felt, knowing what you and her husband did.

7

I have to admit there were times where I wanted to do tic for tac and call up a guy, go get with him and video it so my husband would see how I felt. We all know that never makes things better, so I had no choice but to leave it in God's hands. See it's important to think about the consequences of our actions, because you really do reap what you sow. Most of the time it comes back on you harder than ever.

Everyone thought we would be another divorced couple, but God said no. We stayed in and fought with each other, not against each other. So many people ask how did you do it? I always say it was the Lord's doing. I cried many days and nights. I was embarrassed. I felt alone, I even started to feel those old childhood memories pop back up making me go into a depression. I was determined to not let the enemy defeat us this time. I had to suffer a little but God brought us out smoke free and we are living and loving each other more and more daily.

If there is any lesson to learn, it would be anything worth having is worth fighting for. It doesn't matter the mistakes made, how much hurt and/ or pain that has been caused, it can still work after trauma. Will it be easy? No it will not, but it will be worth it. Marriage is sacred and is honorable by God at a level unexplainable. Marriage requires a lot of forgiveness and apologies, so if you aren't willing to show mercy, it may not be for you. I'm not saying let your spouse cheat and mistreat you, but get on your knees and pray to God to heal, deliver and set free. Also search yourself to make sure you haven't done anything to cause any mishaps in your marriage. It takes two to make marriage work and if you want your marriage to last, keep God at the center and he will definitely guide you through. My husband and I have a motto and we share it with other couples and stand strong on it #NoMoreFailedMarriages. We will share our story and help other couples do marriage God's way and live happily.

Note

The Wake up

By Taisha' Nichole

There is a time when you really have to be prepared when making life changes.

I was so excited to be marrying the man of my dreams and who I would have described as my "Knight in shining armor." I will be honest in saying at one point there were times I felt a little smothered. So, I acted out sometimes instead of communicating. Immaturity! I thought that when I was told "forever "it meant just that, and love would be the reason it would manifest.

There are so many reasons people may get married. Love, money, security, insecurity, being forced, kids, etc. My top reasons were love and security in being loved. I would hear my friends say all the time how they admired our marriage due to their interactions and encounters with us.

The fact that this was all new and there was not much time to really focus on the health of the marriage things didn't last "forever".

The "Wake up" for me was that love doesn't play the role that we think it does because we equate it to a feeling. Love in the blissful, chocolate coated lollipops, blue butterflies, and pink bunny fairy tales that we see on TV isn't really that way. There are going to be obstacles that challenge your words and come against your feelings. There will be people in your ear trying to sabotage what's grown by their poisonous thoughts and opinions. In the thick of things and in the toughest storms is when the word you so freely use is put to the test. There is never a day that your faith won't be pricked with the needle of possible doubt trying to pierce the inner core of its existence. I thought I was invincible. But when two flawed individuals come together as one, there is a mindset that has to shift.

Becoming one doesn't mean you are a half and half to become whole. It's supposed to be two wholes coming together to make "One". Whatever that looks like for each individual marriage may differ. However, the way to figure that out is through proper counseling, having the right people around you who will genuinely hold you BOTH accountable, and both being willing to be wise enough to take in sound wisdom.

The "Wake up" is when you realize that love is actually a word of action, a word you have to choose to act upon daily. Love is an action choice. For example, God loved us enough that he acted upon it by giving us his only son. He had to choose to give something to prove his love and act on it. Jesus too made the choice to love us by enduring much pain and giving his life. All action. The question here is when will you experience the "Wake Up"? When will your love stretch its arms and allow the sun to beam in on its face? When will your Love move out of bed and begin to operate? Wake up!!!! Wipe the sleep out of your love's eyes, roll out of bed, began to step itself onto the floor of respect, put on shoes of responsibility, cloak itself with accountability, put on its ring of trustworthiness, brush it's head with temperance, tuck in some patience, grab a cup of kindness mixed with honesty, and grab a taste of integrity to begin it's effort of daily choice.

I encourage you today to choose to Wake up your Love. Wake up the very being of the action word that has formed the very world we occupy. No, love doesn't pay the bills, but it gives understanding and wants to work hard. Love will make you want to right wrongs and change things that you know can be better. Love will cause you to be in tune with when you're wrong and be honest enough to deal with you, "the real you".

Marriage is a vow, a covenant, and I say the closest intimate relationship equivalent to your relationship with God that you will get with a human being. There is so much power in it. When you can master the art of waking up love daily and making it your choice you will last.

There is so much to this I can touch on. But I will leave you with this! My experience is a testimony of how "The Wake Up" stopped happening. Please be accountable for you. I say all the time "we are only responsible for ourselves". There comes a time that we also have to realize that there is balance where one is weak, the other is strong. I found that I didn't show enough in action the love that was felt. Love is an action word sis. Learn to communicate, be quiet, settle and Wake up!

Note

Married to the Business

By Constance Purnell

As long as I can remember I Have always dreamed of having my own business. At one point in time I thought I would join the military. God knew he had a different path set for my life. (at the age of 12 I started doing my hair at home). I Must have done a damn good job because after that I was doing my sister's hair and my mom's hair and all my cousins and aunts and the girls in the neighborhood. Every morning mom would wake me up at 5 o'clock to do her and my sister's hair before going to school. I will always make sure they were straight and from that led up to me have a small clientele at a young age. the girls at school would say who did your hair and I will say I did.

So after school I will have girls lined up to get their haircut by the time I was 15. I was already known for doing short haircuts! My mom noticed that I had a talent and a gift. And she signed me up for hair school where they offered it at my high school. Who knew 32 years later I will still be in the hair business, having my own hair care product, hair line, Hot tools products and owning my own hair salon for 28 years. But (ladys) let me explain to you how I became married to the business.

Well where do I start to date a young man that was in the same industry as myself. No he was not a barber or hair stylists, but he was a distributor that serviced cosmetologists the best hair care product from Baltimore to South Carolina.

Knowing that we were in the same industry I just knew that we would be compatible. We have so many things in common and the only thing I could dream of would be that we could take over the industry together as a power couple. After dating for two years then we got married. But what I didn't realize is how my dreams would be shattered because of so many disappointments. After seven years of us being married I think that our lives became a competition instead of a marriage there were times that I felt like I had to always prove myself to him, instead of trying to prove it to myself. As years went by he got big in the industry and I got bigger, It put a strain on our marriage. There were times I went to bed and cried myself to sleep because all I wanted was for him to see my worth, how we could have made it together successfully. Instead of us fighting against each other all the time the craziest thing is that all I ever wanted was for him to say you did good honey I'm so proud of you. But I never got those words, so ladies when you are in a marriage and you're not equally yoked It can be very hard. You begin to start feeling like you are alone in your marriage. The one thing that I never wanted was to feel like I am stuck in a situation that I can't get out of and at some point I can't breathe. That truly means a lot to be on the same path in life with your spouse, life will flow so much easier. At one point in my life I feel as if I was my husband's little secret, of course no woman wants to feel that way. What I mean by that lady's is, when in a marriage you start feeling like the SIDE CHICK. Never been asked to major events and never get it acknowledgment. When that started happening I went into a shutdown mood.

That's when survival kicked in for me I started to focus on my brand and making sure that I get my business in order because when you are sleeping with the enemy you have to be proactive and prepare for your next level in life with or without your spouse. I seek God concerning a lot of things, I ask him to help me through this time. It's hard when you're dealing with someone that's fighting against you instead of fighting with you. The lesson that I learned from this lady's is to keep pushing, keep striving to be the best that you can be with the help of God. There have been times when close family and friends have kept me from being suicidal, and going into a state of depression. Sometimes I found myself talking to myself saying girl you are built for this and God made you a strong black queen. I felt at 34 to get married because my biological clock was ticking and most women feel as if you're not married by their 30s all is lost and that you have failed as a woman. I'm here to tell you girl, if you can wait just wait and allow God to send you someone that will love you unconditionally and I will have your back and support you in everything that you do trust me your life will be so much better.

Note

The Cost of Ambiguity

By Raynotta Marie Brooks

Ambiguity: the quality or state of being ambiguous especially in meaning; uncertainty.

In the spring of 2018, around April, I had been in the midst of searching for a home to purchase. My hopeful plan was to have a home secured and closed on before August of that year. I had moved out of my 2 bedroom apartment at the end of March and had been living with a cousin of mine while going through this home buying process. It wasn't the most ideal of situations, but I was very optimistic because I knew that I would be in my own home in just a few months. I had worked hard the past 2 years to clean up my credit, save money and pay down debt. And although I wasn't completely happy with my job, I had planned to remain there long enough to finish the home purchase and save some more money. Thereafter, I would seek more fulfilling employment. Also, the sense of community I was beginning to build within my church was amazing. Life was pretty ok for my 12 year old son and I. Yes, you could say I was content for the most part. I had settled in my heart that marriage must not be what God wanted for me. After all, the love of my life walked away years ago. He made appearances from time to time in my life through those last 6 years, but he just wasn't ready for marriage. I didn't know if he ever would be. And according to the book of Raynotta, there certainly couldn't be anyone else God had for me. Why would I say that you ask? Because I was tainted. A regretful mistake from my past made me feel as if no one else would ever want me if they knew the truth about me. So, I hid behind the false reality that I was ok being single. By doing this, little did I know that I was hindering my healing and my growth. Never allow your past to define you. You are not your mistakes. Jesus died for every mistake and He healed every part of you physically and emotionally before the damage was ever done. You are enough and nothing you have done can't taint you in the eyes of your Daddy. There is more to your story and you don't have to settle for less than God's absolute best for you.

One day, I got the notion to call him. The man that I had been in love with for the past 6 years at that point. We had reconnected briefly months before when he popped up after months of silence, which was customary for him to do from time to time. This is an absolute no, no! Never allow anyone open access to come and go in and out of your life. If a man hasn't seen that you are his wife within the first 2 years and makes a commitment to marry you within a reasonable timeframe, then move on. He doesn't want you sis. This time the call led to deep conversation that opened a door. My heart became open to him once again. Then began the ambiguity. An uncertainty that I would continue to waft away like smoke filled air. Fast forward to May 10, 2018. I received a text from him asking me if I would marry him.

I was shocked. The one thing that I wanted so much had finally happened yet, it was ironically terrifying. After what I claimed as logical thought, I said yes. The next few months were frustrating. The move to my fiancé's home state of Georgia wasn't as easy as I thought it would be. I couldn't seem to land a job. That was likely God telling me to slow my roll, but I saw it as an obstacle to overcome. When faced with obstacles that block something that you desire, then it's likely time to take a long pause and hear from the Father. What is He trying to tell you at that moment? Fast forward to that September after I finally landed a job, we were headed to the courthouse to get married. It felt nothing like I thought it would. My fiancé had become cold and distant during the weeks leading up to the wedding. Maybe things would be different once the formalities of getting married we're behind us. Things certainly did not improve. Small disagreements became huge blow ups that would result in us going days and weeks in silence toward one another. Just 3 months into my marriage I felt extremely unappreciated and unhappy. There were arguments I could have deescalated but I always felt like I had to get my point across. Something I learned from those petty arguments is if it's not a deal breaker then

it's not worth arguing over. If the matter won't matter in a year then let it go. I began praying for my marriage like I should have prayed before I got married. The last argument that broke the proverbial straw happened New Year's Day 2019. We were both at fault. We were both hurt and unhappy and he moved out a few days later without discussion. My heart was so broken I wanted to ask God to just take me; just end my life. As months passed, we went through the motions of trying to work things out again. He'd come and go and so went my heart. That's right, you guessed it, more ambiguity.

My emotions went through rises and falls each time. This was a point that I had to realize that it was only God that was holding me together.

Finally, I made the decision to move my son and I back to South Carolina. After all, my husband already filed for a divorce. This was one of the hardest decisions I've ever had to make. Always be willing to walk away when a man violates those standards and values. This is specifically important in the dating stages because it can eliminate many headaches early on. Unfortunately, I overlooked so much that I now realize were apparent before the marriage.

Making the decision to leave made me feel defeated and worthless. But God had me in His hands the whole time. My husband claimed that he would move to South Carolina as well to work on our marriage. But more ambiguity followed that statement. When I asked when he was coming or wanted to discuss the plans of him moving he avoided the subject by getting angry. Well, that ship of hope quickly sailed away about a month after I arrived in South Carolina. I was devastated. Now I had no choice. I had to make the decision not to wallow in defeat. I had to get up and show up everyday, even when it was hard, even when I felt like I couldn't breathe because my heart was breaking. As I leaned into the pain and faced it head on, my heavenly Father met me right where I was. The moral of this story: Set standards and stick to them. Your willingness to stick to your standards can run away the loser men and will cause the real men to stand out. So when faced with ambiguity especially in a relationship as important as marriage, always seek clarity. And who better to give clarity that the Father. Get quiet, lean in to His heartbeat and follow the rhythm He has set for Your life.

Note

Perfect Love

By Terronda L. Jackson

As a young girl I had many dreams. I dreamed of a perfect childhood, perfect parents, and "perfect love". However, all that I encountered was let down after let down. Absolutely nothing was perfect about my life. Who was I to think I deserved anything perfect anyway?

Like every young girl I dreamed of falling in love, being swept off my feet by my perfect knight in shining armor. I envisioned the perfect wedding, the big house with the white picket fence. Of course I'd already planned to create the perfect family, with 2 children, a boy and a girl to complete my perfect little family portrait. In a perfect world this is how my life would have unfolded. Unbeknownst to me, I'd never see the perfect family that I imagined in my head. On the contrary my childhood was full of rejection, hurt, pain, trauma, abandonment and way too many disappointments to list.

The truth is none of us grew up in a perfect world. There is no perfect childhood and there are no perfect parents. There most certainly is no perfect love, save one, which I didn't discover until much later in life. My truth is there was no fairytale wedding or perfect knight in shining armor. There was no home with a white picket fence and there certainly was no perfect life, no perfect love.

I was raised in a single-parent home. My teen mother later became hooked on drugs and struggled to take care of me. The father that I longed for my entire life had moved thousands of miles away to the opposite side of the country before I was even born. Who was I to think I was worthy of a "perfect love" from any man, let alone a perfect knight in shining armor? Who was I to think that I deserved true love when my own father didn't want me, didn't love me, didn't even care for me?

My childhood was so unfruitful that it left me broken, barren, bitter, unbalanced, and naive.

My identity was bound to be in question from birth. My original foundation was virtually nonexistent and what little that was there was very unstable. The validity of my existence never claimed and overshadowed by lack from day one. I did not have the relationship nor the connection to the two people who were assigned to mold and shape my life. I did not have the appropriate connection with my mother who was supposed to nurture, love, and teach me to be a young lady. I felt no significance to the woman who gave me life and was assigned to breathe life into me. I did not have the covering from my father who was supposed to love, support, encourage, protect, and cover me. This hurt me and damaged me

34

as a person, as a human, as a young woman. I had no idea who I was. I needed my parents. I just wanted to be loved. That was all.

The dream of a perfect life, a perfect marriage, and a perfect love died right along with my identity. I felt as though I was birthed by mistake. I only grew older because I had no choice. Once I came to the realization surrounding my existence I was crushed. What little self-love I did have slowly dissipated the older I became. Continued periods of rejection from my Father chipped away at me until there was nothing left but a shell of who I was supposed to be. There was nothing, no "I love You's", no lessons about how a young lady should be treated, just nothing. I felt unlovable, unwanted, and inadequate. Many times, I reached out to my Father, but he hardly ever responded. So many empty promises and lies. He never came when he said he was coming, and the birthday gifts and Christmas gifts never arrived in the mail. For years following I found myself repeating the childhood narrative of being abandoned and rejected by my Father over and over. My heart and mind were sick. I attracted exactly what I was, sick and unhealthy. This left me unable to maintain meaningful connections and relationships, especially with the opposite sex. I wouldn't have recognized an emotionally healthy man if my life depended on it.

I moved with my mother and we attempted to build our relationship. My mother gave her life to Christ and I started going to church with my mother. Slowly the layers of hurt and pain started to shed away from my heart and mind. I could vaguely see the light of God. He was showing me just who I was. Some things I liked and others I did not. Over the next few years, it was painful dealing with my ugly truths, but It was necessary.

It was working and I was feeling better about myself, so I kept pushing. My self-confidence was rising, and I was feeling good about myself.

I eventually went to college and I was feeling very accomplished with my coursework. While attending college I met a young man and we became very good friends. We started dating the next year and were married the following year. It seemed as though everything was falling in place for me. Was this God? Had I really met and married my perfect knight in shining armor? Even though this was a happy time, I was secretly struggling to maintain connection. I felt like I was losing myself again. Most of the time I was ok and I could hide what was wrong. Inside I was an emotional wreck which left me feeling incompetent in my marriage. I buried my feelings and avoided facing my truths and dealing with reality. I was reverting and I was scared I would lose everything.

Slowly but surely the past began to creep up on me. I began to doubt myself. I doubted God. I doubted my husband's love for me. I questioned everything. How can I love my husband when I don't love myself? After all, I don't even know what love is. The insecurities were so great that I sank to an all time low. I felt unlovable. I had become content in the lowly place and my self-esteem plummeted. I once again had forgone my birthright to love and be loved because I could not identify my heart's posture. I was going through the motions, but unhappy and unfulfilled in myself and in my marriage. I had allowed the enemy to rob me of myself again.

Each time I looked into my husband's loving face all I could think about was how my father deserted me and that he never came back. The first man who was supposed to love me, in fact obligated to love me, deserted me, and I was sure that my husband would leave too. I found myself being a wife; but the little girl in me was yet screaming for love, acceptance, and attention. I so desperately wanted to be the wife he deserved and the mother that my children needed me to be. I really wanted to be her, but I didn't know how, and I had no idea where to start.

I wanted someone, or something to just fix me. I knew I had to shake this mindset and change the way I saw myself. I was truly at the end of myself. All avenues had been exhausted. There was nowhere else to go, but back to God. It was then at my lowest point I acknowledged that I had no idea who I was or what I believed anymore. I was compelled to fully submit to God. I was compelled to acknowledge my flaws, my faults, and my shortcomings. For the first time in my life I admitted that I was afraid.

You cannot overcome what you will not acknowledge. I acknowledged everything. I told the truth and I was honest with my husband about what I had been experiencing and why I had been acting a certain way. Guess what? He forgave me and he didn't leave me. He didn't walk away. He stayed and he helped me to fight. He prayed with me and for me. He covered me and he made me feel safe. He believed in me. He trusted me. He helped me to find me again. I finally had a safe place to take a step back, reevaluate my life, and identify where this irrational thought pattern began. Where did the struggle with "self" enter my life? Where was the portal opened? How do I move on from here?

I now had a name for it. I acknowledged it and I was ready to face it and ready to fight for my identity. I needed to stop this curse dead in its tracks to find out who I was. I realized that sometimes we go through hard things to make us stronger. There were times when I felt like I wasn't going to make it. I questioned God in the midst of it, but I kept moving and didn't quit. I kept trusting and believing in the process. It got better with each passing day. Yes, it was rough at times, but I got through it. Yes, it was unpleasant, but I have learned so much, not just about myself, but also about others and I am better because of it.

I was now able to stand on my own two feet. I no longer look to others for identity or purpose. I found my identity in God. I no longer think of myself as weak because it is in my weakness that God's strength is made perfect. I no longer look outside of myself for validation. My heavenly Father validates me. I am my own woman and I know who I am in God. I stopped looking through the lens of man and depending on irrational beliefs. I now view myself and others through the lens of God. I am now able to cast now every imagination that tries to exalt itself against my identity in Christ.

I never achieved the perfection that I dreamed of and I'm ok with that. I actually stopped searching for it and I started hiding. I hid myself in prayer. I hid myself in the word. I simply hid myself in God, the deeper I went and the more consistent I was the more my true, authentic self was revealed. The truth made me free.

I didn't find perfection in my mother, my father, my sister, or my brother. I didn't find it in the clubs or the dance hall. I didn't find it in the drugs and alcohol or the cigarettes, but I found it in Jesus Christ the Righteous. He is the "Perfect Love".

"Hide yourself, to find yourself."

My Truths:

My identity was never lost, but merely hidden in God.

When I found out who God was, I found out who I was.

I have a Father who loves me immensely and treasures me deeply.

My past experiences do not determine my future.

I am not responsible for the actions of others, but mine alone.

All things really do work for my good. (If it's not good, then God isn't done with it yet.)

I am "beautifully broken" and always wonderfully made.

My stumbling blocks are my stepping stones.

Scriptures:

Such love has no fear, because perfect love expels all fear. If we are afraid, it is for fear of punishment, this shows that we have not fully experienced his perfect love. 1John 4:18, NLT

The Lord himself goes before you and will be with you; he will never leave you nor forsake you. Do not be afraid; do not be discouraged. Deuteronomy 31:8, NIV

And we know that God causes everything to work together for the good of those who love God and are called according to his purpose for them. Romans 8:28, NLT

Not only so, but we also glory in our sufferings, because we know that suffering produces perseverance; perseverance, character; and character, hope. And hope does not put us to shame, because God's love has been poured out into our hearts through the Holy Spirit, who has been given to us. Romans 5:3-5, NIV

Casting down imaginations, and every high thing that exalteth itself against the knowledge of God, and bringing into captivity every thought to the obedience of Christ. 2 Corinthians 10:5 KJV

Then you will know the truth, and the truth will set you free. John 8:32, KJV

Note

The Continuous Vow

By Tonya Lewis-Rose

For better or worse, sickness or health, richer or poorer to death do we part. To have to hold and to honor that's what we vowed. But what happens when life happens and we have to live out those words. How do you still choose to live this life when those words have little power? When the validity of the marriage is questioned by the actions of those who vowed. I can recall the days of dying inside because of the woman that stood at the altar at 20 yrs old she had no clue of what was ahead of her. The happiness, the sadness, the failures, the triumphs and the choices she would have to make on a daily basis! The times when you have to secretly cry yourself asleep because of the void of being heard. The void of feeling honored. As time continued, I began to understand that the real struggle was not the marriage, not the failures I made, not the spouse, but the inability to choose properly. No one ever truly teaches us before marriage how to learn the balance of being a wife. How to daily make the vow to be devoted to motherhood, partnership and yourself. It really is possible. Although, we might make mistakes and have to endure heartache and pains. It is still possible. But it does require realigning our thoughts and actions with what our heart desires. It takes confidence in you. It requires you to continue to vow and commit to the process of marriage. Confidence in that a marriage does not define who you are. Rather here or there, who you are today is who you chose to be. It's who you vow to be! Why do we have to go through so much before we see the worth in who we are. Beyond your mistakes, beyond the molestation, regardless of the disappointments and fears. God has a purpose and plan to prosper you and bring you to an expected end.

How is it that we can be the life giver to so many, but die within our own promise? The promises of God stand sure! God knows them that belong to him. He knows your heart. He knows you're hurt. He knows how to position you and place you in momentum to prosper. In prosperity it's not just about finances. It covers the posture of your heart. God is concerned about what concerns you. It doesn't matter what is going on in the world. When we depend and lean on him, he will come and see about you. Sometimes in making the right choice every day we have to choose our significant others. That's where the work begins. Because we are bound by the experiences that we have encountered. He knows how to reach the deep things in our heart. Those things that hold us hostage. He is our advocate. In those times we can't fight for ourselves. Those times we feel no one can see us or hear us. He is fighting for you! The help is in how you choose. He knows how to break every chain in our lives. Chains of depression, defeat, anxiety, timidity and chains of lack emotionally and physically.

When we give those things to God. He will rescue you and keep you from retracting backwards. He knows how to heal the hurt places in our life. When we choose us. We can never be denied access to what God has for us. The marriage will survive, the home will thrive, the vision will come to pass, and the hurt will be healed. When we choose us. We can come boldly to the throne and obtain mercy in our times of need. There is a place that we can go. Sometimes we feel no one ever truly understands. No one can relate to the turmoil that goes on in the mind. The perplexity of the choices. When the power of God comes. Those chains are destroyed. It can't be done in our own might. Through him he will perform miracles. You must choose you. Your future and family are waiting and hoping in your choice. As women because we are such nurturers by design. We often continue to nurture things that are intended to die. We want to save the world. And, when we see that we can't save the world, we drown in the feeling of guilt, insufficiency and low-self esteem. Everybody expects us to have the solution and to know the answer. When in truth like our spouses, friends and children. So often we are searching for the same answers they are. In the midst of the search we just know how to hold things together. Sometimes the one thing we hold the tightest is ourselves. We hold our emotions, our self-worth, our dignity and our voice. I offer to you a better way today. It's okay to choose you. It's okay to decide this is what I will do for me. I promise once you do, you will see that God is who is needed in all those issues you're trying to sacrifice you for. The only real difference is him. When we step away, he steps up! Make the choice to choose you. Stand tall in that choice. Be humble in your position and allow the power God to mend what's broken. You must choose him daily. The price has been paid for our liberty and freedom. He's provided a way to him even in the midst of destruction. Those pieces that can't even be found in the shipwreck. God knows exactly where they are.

Sometimes things can be in such disarray mostly within us. We don't possess the clarity of thought and peace in our heart or mind to see him in the midst of the brokenness. He can and will put those pieces back together. He will establish your goings. Giving you a new hope and brand-new identity in him. He will provide a hope and a future because you dared to trust him and to choose you. After all, he lives in you! In the end we will see that he was always able. He will reaffirm our belief by the sight of his ability. When we almost gave up, no strength to endure. He will give us our belief back, when we choose him. His hope and deliverance live on the inside of you. Choose you and work on you. Forget the faults, failures, hurts and disappointments. Focus on the future and the power of the moment that you live in right now. In this very moment, despite what you feel or see. God is right there with you. He is keeping you. Holding you and wiping your tears. He is directing you in all your ways. He is so mighty and all powerful. He made you and all that he ever made was good! Like me I had to learn that this vow must be made daily. No matter how tough it gets, how dark the days become or how lost you might find yourself at times. You too must continuously make the vow. Choose you, because you too matter! Learn the value in who you are. Before Mrs. or before the mommy. God made you who you are. There is treasure in you. What the enemy wants to display as insufficient. He declares that it's more than enough. He knows how to stretch and multiply what you have. To make it greater and bigger! The vow was always so much for than either you or your spouse could ever know. That's the mystery of who God is. When we stay in the vow, he stays in us. He blesses us because it's his good pleasure to give you the KINGDOM! Continue to make the vow!

Note

Motherhood

Why Not?

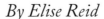

By Elise Reid

When I experienced a traumatic loss of my son at 7 months into my pregnancy, I grieved and did not understand. However, someone very close to me began losing faith and questioning God because they were grieving for me and losing my son. 15 years of battling infertility and my son is taken away. It was after a conversation that I had with God that I had a better understanding. I gave this same information to her and although it is seemingly harsh, it is the truth. After reading it her faith was restored and I became stronger because of what God put in my heart. I would like to share with you what God told me ten years ago. It's not just about the loss of a child, but a loss of any kind. A relationship, a marriage, death of a loved one, health, and more can be a loss. These words that God gave me have helped bring me through all the losses I have experienced through the years. I wish I had known this for the 15 years prior to knowing because I believe it would have helped me make some better decisions.

You never really know how strong you are until you go through something. You don't know how strong a house is until a storm comes. There are different types of storms that we encounter in our lives. Most of the time we go through storms. Although they seem strong at the time, when it's over and the sun shines bright we realize, yes it was bad, but we came through. But then there comes the worst storm we have ever encountered. A storm so strong that it reads off the Richter scale. It's the storm that will either make us or break us. If we make it through the storm, we come out alive but hurting. If we give up, we either die or lose a very core part of us.

When others see us going through a storm, they tell us to trust God and he'll make a way. Everything is for a reason. Put your faith in God and he'll see you through. I'm praying for you. Things we usually don't want to hear. We want people to either shut up and just leave us alone or just be honest. Tell us, sis, your situation is bad. There is no telling when things will get better and I honestly can't tell you why it's happening, God's reason or not. Faith just doesn't seem enough to help you. But I promise you if you just hold on, this too will pass.

God said you are feeling nothing worse than I have ever felt. I had to turn my back on my own son due to the sin he had to take on. I watched him in extreme pain and although I wanted to save him, heal him, and take away his pain I would not. It's not that I could not but I would not. It tore my heart when he cried out to me and said, "Abba (Father) why have you forsaken me?"

Don't you think I cried? If I created you in my image, don't you think I feel pain just as I created you to feel pain. In the garden, he asked me to take away his suffering to come. I did not respond although I wanted to just save him. I could have wiped out those who persecuted him. The ones who whipped him until his flesh tore away from his body. The one who pierced him in his side. The one who even offered him vinegar to drink like it was funny. When they put each nail in his body and he screamed out in agony. When each drop of his precious blood was drained from his body. When they thrust the crown of thorns on his head and caused him more pain. I wanted to protect him, but I would not because of the purpose he had.

Or the pain that I feel each day that one of my creations turns their back on me and rejects me. The ones who serve me wholly each day and then backslide. The ones who stumble and can't seem to find their way although my hand is right there to lead them. To see the ones who reject my grace, mercy, and salvation after watching my son go through all the ridicule and pain, to die for their sins. Even more so when each day more of my creation is being put in hell. I can hear their screams of pain and agony. I can see the anguish on their faces. The ones pleading to me to save them and promising to change if given another chance. Sadly, I know their hearts and know that if given another chance it would not matter. When Adam and Eve, my first creation turned their backs on me by being disobedient, don't you think that hurt me? When I looked for them in the garden and they were hiding, don't you know I already knew what they had done? I saw Eve talking to the serpent, I saw Eve taste the apple. I also saw when Adam, listening to the woman I created for him taste the apple too. It hurt me when I had to curse them and throw them from the garden. The spiral of sin and death they began that infected my entire human race. David, who was a man after my own heart, the warrior, the prayer, and the psalmist. He turned his back on me by committing adultery and having Bathsheba's husband killed to have her. That hurt me. It even hurt me when I had to take his newborn son.

You're no more special than Job who I allowed the devil to take everything from him but his life. Would you rather be in his place? But despite the suffering I allowed him to go through, although he was a righteous man in my sight, he did not curse me or turn his back on me. Instead he still loved me. In return I blessed him many times over.

My word says that "*For* surely, I know the plans I have for you... *plans for your welfare and not for harm, to give you a future with hope.*" This means I can see past what you cannot. I can see past your pain that is blinding you right now. You ask me why did I allow this to happen? My question... is why not? Do you believe that life should always be painless? Do you think you are not supposed to go through trials and tribulations? My son did. And the reason he did was FOR YOU. Six months from now, will you be stronger? What about a year? If I let you know why I did it, would it make the pain go away? Will it make the burden more bearable? If I took away your unborn child and you asked me why and I told you that it was to take the place of your oldest child who was going to die in a car accident, would you feel better? No, you would ask me why I couldn't just save them both. Everything I do IS for a reason. It does not make you feel better, but it is true. I do not take my decisions lightly. I do not allow things to happen to hurt you. If you truly trust me when things are good, why can't you do the same when things are bad? I made one as well as the other.

From this revelation I learned that my loss, traumatic as it was, is nothing in comparison to God's loss that he goes through everyday. It is nothing compared to others who have lost far more than I ever have or will. There is always someone going through more than me and I would rather stay in my shoes than walk in theirs. "God does everything for a reason" is not comforting at all. However, it is true. Two years after our loss God gave us a miracle daughter and although I still miss my son, God gave me a gift in her. Your loss right now feels eternal, but hold on to what I said because it will get better. Your loss is your testimony to pass on to help someone else.

Note

Side Chick

What Goes Around Comes Around

By Ondia Wyatt Petty

I can remember always hearing people say, "Watch how you treat people, because it will come back on you some way or another." The only thing is I never thought things would or could come back on me the way they did. See I was your typical young mother of four, working as a CNA, with my own section8 housing, a nice car, and I took care of myself. My children's fathers were living the street life, so you know how that goes. Yeah I was the INDEPENDENT hood chick!!

I grew up in a dysfunctional Christian home if that makes sense. I went to church faithfully Monday through Sunday, but at home that love of God was not shown. Therefore, I developed a lot of unhealthy personality traits. I was angry, evil, bitter, low self-esteem, lacked appropriate verbal communication, a liar, and a thief. I became sexually curious due to being touched on by women and men. And so much more happened that turned me into a toxic person.

One day in 2011, I met a man that I knew was married and we began to talk and things got a little deep and intense. My conscience didn't kick because I just didn't care about the consequences of my actions. I enjoyed the attention he gave me. I loved the fact I controlled when we talked and when we didn't. I never asked him to do anything but he would volunteer to do things for me and my children and I would gladly accept. He would come take me on dates in his and his wife's car. One day for Valentine's Day he took me to their house. He always said he was leaving his wife to be with me because I was his peace and life would be so much better with me.

Blah blah blah!! I mean I listened but I wasn't trying to hear all that. Just come through get me off and go on about your day. I mean he would do everything under the sun to me and I would let him. I was a selfish side chick. I mean, I knew he was going home to her while thinking about me and kissing her after he just left me. But my bills were paid and I was living the dream life. I wasn't thinking about how that man was going to do the same thing to me if we were together. Oh so I failed to inform you that he was a minister and a major leader in the church I attended. My children knew him and would see him at my house and church. I would tell them, "who you see in this house, you don't know them if we see them out in public!!" In other words, what goes in this house, stays in this house and if you open your mouths, I will beat your behinds.

I was active in the music department, so I would see him every time I went to church. Sometimes we'd be in service and I'd feel him looking at me, so I'd look down and his wife would be staring and smiling at me like "Hey Girlll!!" I would tell him how uncomfortable I was getting, but by this time, we were "In love" and I was in too deep so I thought. He wasn't listening to me because he thought he had me wrapped to the point I wouldn't leave.

By this time my Holy Ghost has started to tap in. This is not right and I knew I had to let it go. I just didn't know how to do it. I prayed and asked God for strength. So here we are years in this thing, he's still married, still telling me he's leaving, and I'm still sitting around looking dumb. Even though I started the relationship cold hearted, my walls broke down and I became vulnerable to what I knew wasn't right.

One night at revival the word was so life changing, the spirit was high, and God got a hold of me like never before. He texted me during service and said, "You're so beautiful!!! I love you!!" I responded, "I'm done!!! I can't do this anymore." I saw the look on his face and his whole mood changed as if I had just broken his heart. He responded, "but why?" I told him it wasn't right. I was burdened down by this sin and as children of God we know better. I had to come to church week after week, smiling in his wife and children's faces, being fake, acting like a big hypocrite.

I had begun to think I wasn't good enough and that settling was my only option. I had been living in sin, fear, and bondage so long that I had forgotten about the word of God spoken over my life. I had forgotten to speak life in my dead situations. I woke up one day and I began to die to my flesh, pleading the blood of Jesus over mine and my children's lives, because not only had I opened myself up to darkness, but my children as well. I had forgotten that which you sow, you shall also reap! I immediately got on my knees and repented for my actions and thoughts and asked the Lord to save me once again.

I knew there was a calling on my life and the route I was heading was not beneficial to me fulfilling God's purpose and plan. When I sent that text to tell him it was over we never talked again and I felt a burden lift off of me that night. I didn't question how it was so easy to let go, I just did it. Anything God ordains he will maintain and being the chick to another woman's husband was not God's intentions for my life.

The greatest lesson to learn from this "Side Chick" lifestyle is it's better to wait on the one God tailor made for you. No matter how much attention you get from the other person, they're still going home to someone else, giving the same attention they gave you. You're worth more than being an option!!!

Note

Single Mother

The Struggle of a mother with twins

By Constance Purnell

O h wow! Where do I begin? I am Constance Purnell and in 1992 I became a single mother of twin boys to be exact. Jeremy Danyel Lewis was born 3 minutes before Joshua Denzel Lewis and at this time my world had just changed. At the age of 24, I just delivered twin boys on March 8, 1992, a day after my birthday. I was very young becoming a mother of two. After dating their father for 3 years, having to go through the ups and downs, the lying, cheating, and heartbreak that I endured at that time; the only thing I could think about were my sons and how to show them double love. Because now I have to be the mother and the father. Now knowing I can only teach them how to love, honor, and take care of a woman. But of course, I would never be able to teach them how to be a man.

I do believe the hardest time in my life was facing the fact that I was going to be a single parent. I continued just to work hard in my business and at that time the name of my salon was O'Neal's Hair Studio. I had a very flourishing business and clientele, so I was able to maintain it with the help of my family and take care of my sons alone. I tried to go back and date their father again. But that didn't work out good. I remember lying down after putting my sons to bed and they were only 10 months old. There was a knock at the door, and it was a young lady asking for my kids' father. This lady was in so much rage till she kept knocking and knocking louder. I asked my kids father, "do you hear the knock at the door?" He said, "no Constance, just lay down, I hear nothing." The lady continuously knocked and yelled out his name. I then proceeded to get up and answer the door. From that day forward I knew that I could never go back to my children's father again. The lady began to share with me how she had been into my apartment before and how she had made love in that same apartment with my boyfriend. My heart was so crushed. He stormed out of the bedroom and began to attack the lady because of what she was telling me. Finally, I was able to get her out of the apartment and I called the police. But before the police could get there, she had run her car into his. That made his car crash into the windows of our apartment. All because he wanted to try to date two women. I learned a valuable lesson that night. I lost all trust in men and that I had to turn into survival mode for me and my kids.

After I left him, I never looked back. I decided not to date for a while and just focus on my children and my business. Shortly after I met a young man that just totally swept me off my feet and he had nothing but love for me and my children and my family. When I tell you that I fell deeply in love with this young man, it was just so surreal. He took such good care of me and my children, so I didn't even pay attention about what he did for a living or that I was the side chick. Yes, ladies, you heard me, the side chick. When I found out it was too late. I was already in love. It was hard for me to tell there was anyone else because he was always catering to my wants and needs. He was always there for me too. It had gotten to a point where it didn't matter. I did not have to deal with someone else. See ladies, sometimes I think that when you have children that you got to provide for; you begin to do the unthinkable and you just settle. The craziest thing though is that he was so good to me and I felt like I could win him over. This went on about another year. He ended up getting arrested for selling drugs. You have to remember, this is in the 90's, so that was the biggest thing for men to do, to take care of their family. So he never told me what he did. As a matter of fact, he told me he had his own construction company in New York, and I went with that.

After dealing with that for another year, I decided that I would date again and fell for this young man that was about five years younger than me. He led me to believe that he was three years older than me. But I found out. His mother and I became close. His family accepted my children as their own and I truly loved his family for that. I think what I love about their family is that they were very close knit just like ours. So our relationship lasted pretty long. I just knew he would be my husband but at the time that I had made sure I was ready to go to the next level in life. He was not quite ready yet. I tried to hang on just so my sons had a father figure in their life because again a woman can't raise a man. She can only show him how to love, honor, and to protect his woman. So, now we are up to the present day and I must say

I did a damn good job raising my sons because all they have ever seen was me working hard building my brand and setting goals in life to always reach my highest level. And from that I am proud to announce that my sons are now a part of the beauty industry. They are both barbers. Actually, I thank God for what I have instilled in them. I don't think I did a bad job, thank you God.

Note

Metamorphosis

By ONO

Where do I begin? I wasn't always the best person. I did whatever I felt I was big and bad enough to do. I was a bad child coming up. I gave my mama HELL. I remember asking myself, "why are you so dang gone bad? I would wonder, how was I made? Who made me? I asked myself if I was a puppet, but if I was a puppet, where are the strings that control my limbs and why was I so bad? Nope! I'm not a puppet! Am I a robot? Nope! Cause robots don't have feelings but when I heard about God and Jesus a light switch just turned on!!!! It only made sense! It had to be something supernatural!! Having eyes to see outward instead of inward, a heart that beats, sets the sun in the sky, and the stars and the moon to burn bright at night. This can only be the work of someone great and mighty!! At a young age, I made up in my mind. I believed with my whole heart that Jesus Christ was (still is) the son of God and He gave His son that I might have life. I got baptized at the age of 12 and came up from under that water feeling free. I graduated from high school, got married, and had three sons. Life was good. Then all hell broke loose. I got divorced and hooked up with an old classmate. A total nightmare. I had a son, and now a single mother of four, my gifts from God. Some of the best years of my life. I met the love of my life and never knew love like that before then.

Eleven years later my baby boy started acting up in school. DSS stepped in and took my baby boy. My family and friends said "call your Pastor and talk to him." I didn't have to call him because I realized that I have nothing without Jesus Christ. I went back to church and every single Sunday my Pastor had a Word that I felt was just for me. The Word carried me through the worst six months of my life. While I waited for my baby boy to return, I was growing spiritually. While waiting I didn't have a choice but to take a real good look at myself; I mean a real good look. I have been running for the Lord ever since. I always knew that God is real. My greatest desire is to make sure He is pleased with me and how I treat others. I know that He wants us to love others more because love conquers a multitude of sin. He is the kind of God that loves us just that much. So, if He can love me that much, as bad as I was, I can love others just the same. I realized if you walk with God, you can have whatsoever you ask. After every hardship is a growth spurt. A metamorphosis. It hurts. But as a result, I am stronger, so much better, and so much wiser. God has proven time and time again that when I keep Him first, everything just falls into place. I am TOTALLY persuaded that neither death, nor life, nor angels, nor principalities nor powers, nor things present nor things to come, nor height, nor depth, nor any other creature, shall be able to separate me from the love of God, which is in Christ Jesus our Lord.

Note

The Nuances of Single Motherhood

By Raynotta Marie Brooks

What's your single mom story? There are many nuances to this single mother thing. From the way we became single parents to the type of support from the other parent that may or may not be there for whatever reason. No matter what your single mom story is, you are gifted for the task. You may bend under the pressure and stress that comes with this wonderfully challenging yet rewarding job, but you don't have to break. You see, the breaking point isn't meant to break you, it's meant to purify you. A silversmith's job is to work with pieces of silver until they become pure and refined masterpieces. This is no easy task. The silver is hammered at room temperature and as it is formed, it hardens. At this point in the process it needs to undergo a heat treatment to soften it. If it is not softened by heat, it will weaken, crack and break. Momma, you are a masterpiece! You were not meant to break. Malachi 3:2-3 talks about the Lord being a refiner's fire and purifier of silver. We build thick skin as single mothers because of the things we must endure. Life can certainly harden you. We carry the weight of our world and our children's worlds as if we can do it alone. The Father has to remind us that we can't do it on our own. Life hammers away at us until we reach the breaking point. That's when the refiner steps in with His purifying fire to soften us so that we can be molded into the servants and mothers that He has called us to be. Trials are used to purify our hearts. Left un-purified, our spirits would break. And no child needs a broken momma. The fact is, we all have our moments when we feel as if we are going to break. One particular potentially breaking moment happened to me the morning of November 3, 2019. I had babysat the night before for a sweet couple that I've known for a few years. A night that earned me money toward bills that I couldn't pay. I awoke to a soaking wet carpet in the closet of the room of the 1bedroom apartment my 14 year old son and I shared. There had been a leak going on for weeks that the maintenance staff could not find the source of. I awoke not knowing if I would receive renewed food stamp benefits to buy food for us.

I had just filled out the renewal paperwork to mail in. I awoke to a mounting avalanche of debt that was trying to crush me and an almost daily plummeting credit score. I awoke to a thinly furnished apartment with rent I couldn't afford. I felt like a mess and a failure as a mother. I was a newly single again mom. A mom that had gone from having the somewhat security of a spouse, to now going back to the drawing board. It was at that moment when I felt like I would break that I had to make a decision to either crumble or lean into the heat and allow God to purify and purge me.

So, let me take you back to the beginning of my single mom story. October 25, 2005 I became a mother. I became a mother in a way that I never imagined I would. I envisioned motherhood for me happening in a loving, supportive marriage. I never thought I would welcome a child into the world as a single parent. But, being the independent go-getter I am, I took this nuance of my story and ran with it. The 8 year on again off again relationship/ situationship with my son's father finally ended in 2009. My son was about 3 years old at that time. Upon the ending of that relationship, I dated here and there but I was very selective about bringing men in the presence of my son. Exposing your children to a man that is not their father and that has not made a commitment to marry you can be very damaging. If the relationship doesn't work out, not only do you have to break an emotional soul tie, but now so does that child. I threw myself into the work of raising my amazing son. A son that God had entrusted me with to watch over and groom into a man. His father was and still is in his life, providing financial and emotional support. However, the day to day task of parenting is all in my hands. Upon getting married in September of 2018, I was sure that my single parenting days were behind me. That dream quickly faded a little over a year following my wedding day. As a divorced single again mother, more than ever before, I look to the refiner to soften me under the pressure of the task I've been given.

We must always remember that our children mirror us. If we are confused and aimless in life, they will be as well. If we are allowing people to manipulate and use us, so will they. But, if we show perseverance and strength even through divorce, absence of the other parent or death of a spouse, so will they. You are their first and biggest cheerleader, motivator, teacher, confidant and life coach. It is through your wholeness and healing that they discover the power to walk in the power the Lord has placed inside of them. You momma, have the power to break generational curses. The power to set your children up to not only live their best lives through their God given purpose, but to also know that when adversity strikes, our good, good Father can bring them through it. The Father has placed in us the anointing to be so whole as single mothers that our children won't even feel the lack of a father. Teach them that the absence of their father does not diminish their value. Push the greatness inside of them and let them feel your touch daily. If you're in the fire, lean in to be purified. The Lord is molding a servants' heart within the masterpiece He is creating

Note

Single Mommy x Two

By Taisha' Nichole

As a single mother you want nothing more for your children to be in an environment of happiness and wholeness.

I was a single mom the first time as a jr at Benedict college in Columbia, Sc. I was so ready to start my journey to campaign for Ms. Benedict and have my face in the Ebony magazine. I just knew I had it in the bag. Months before it was time to begin I was feeling weird so I decided to get a test. I took the test and hopped in the shower. Well.... I reached for the towel and saw two lines. I was floored. So in denial I took the test like five more times. I guess I thought the result was going to change. The only thing that changed was my life. I got through the remainder of my year and had to make a choice. Stay 10 hours from home or go back to Ohio. Heck no!!! I said if I had to live on the street I'd never go back home (not knowing I'd have to one day, keep reading).

I had a beautiful little baby girl July 14,2005 one month before my Senior year was to start. My grandmother (mom) had co-signed for me to get an apartment. My Mommy gave me a car and I had to figure the rest out on my own. August 2005 I was back on campus sometimes carrying a car seat going from class to class. Some of my choir family (BCGC) would take her for me and we'd switch up between classes. She was the campus baby, even some of the staff would keep her in their office while I went to class. You see I was working but by the time I went to work and had a friend keep her so I could work I still couldn't afford daycare so I could go to school during the day. By the time I found an in home daycare that would work with me sometimes I was to tired to even take her. It was a struggle, not to mention I was also breastfeeding. Lord help!!!

It got to be overwhelming because I had to retake classes so that I could bring up my gpa. I ended up sending my daughter home for the remainder of my senior year, I was to graduate that December. With my daughter with my family for a few months I was able to finish college and earn my degree.

One thing I gained was that there is a mindset you have to have as a mother to never stop no matter what obstacles come your way. I struggled for a while, but honestly had a pretty solid support system between my aunt who lived here and my Diamond sisters and my family at home. Some faculty members would keep her overnight and meet me at the school with her just to help out. I was blessed beyond measure and grateful, but there were many times I had to just figure it out.

Fast forward 11 years…...Well, sis there was a second time of single motherhood. This time my emotional state was jacked (I'd say insert word here) I was separated from my husband.

This time I had two children (with me) homeless and from pillar to post. Trying to put things back together. Humiliated, broken, hurt, I had to once again figure it out. This time the support system looked a little different. There were a lot of hard times sleeping in other people's houses sometimes on the couch or the floor. Being the single mother this time wasn't as charming this go round. I felt like I failed my children because they began to struggle and there was nothing I could do but support them. I had to cry many nights and pray really hard that I could be who they needed me to be for them. This time I learned the real meaning of mommy. Putting their emotional, physical and spiritual needs where times 100 now. I became even more sensitive to their needs because I was all they had to look to. Once I began to get things back on track I began to realize how important it is to keep my mind on what mattered my children and their wellbeing. I had to stand firm on my faith, my foundation and allow God to show me how to operate.

If I can say anything to a single mother is no matter the struggle or if you have an amazing support system you have to endure the emotional and sometimes physiological aspects of being Mommy. I made up my mind that my children would never go lacking that they would never see their mom take a hit and stay down. I'm teaching them endurance, resilience, grace, strength and above all faith in God. I understand that nothing I've gone through was just for me but it was to help another single mother along the way either single or going through a separation from a spouse. It's at my expense that you will be stronger, better and wiser. I choose to write out my words in my own story "Silent no More" to save the lives of those who turn the pages.

Sis, know that your story has chapters and every chapter ends different. Stay encouraged and remember you were broken to glow, you're a glowstick!

(A glowstick can only serve its purpose if it's broken)

I'm a Mommy x Two but I keep on repeat I'm Possible and you should to. We got this!!!!

Note

My Naked Truth

"Single Parent of #4"
By Angelic O'Neal

My story is filled with broken pieces, troubled choices an ugly truths. It also filled with a major comeback, a peace of mind and Grace that saved my life.

I became a mother at the early age of 17 not truly knowing how to financially take care of myself. Still in high school, trying to put on a front by covering up my embarrassment and shame. My worst fear was telling my parents, not knowing their reaction. Being raised in a Christian based household and attending a holiness Church, had me feeling very condemned and from what I was taught having a baby out of wedlock will send you straight to hell. But having my own relationship with God, allows me to work through my disappointments. #YOUDON'TKNOWMYSTORY...

Regardless of what others thought of me. I remained in high school, finished my 12th grade year, graduated and held down two jobs during the whole process. I consider myself blessed and fortunate enough to have my family love & support with help raising my son.

As time went by, not knowing I will be pregnant again with my daughter a with my daughter a year-and-a-half later. But by this time, my two older siblings and I are sharing a house together. I refused to overthink and went along with the flow. Life situations often have you thinking the absolute worst. At this point all I was thinking is nothing could affect my ability to move forward as a single parent. #YOUDON'TKNOWMYSTORY...

Even with the stumbling block I now have the mindset to fight and get back up.

I often had to remind myself that I have two small people depending on me. Trying not to get in a slump or depend on welfare and child support. I worked hard as I could to take care of what I produce.

I can remember sitting on my parents porch between the age of 11/13 still playing with doll babies, and now being a single parent of three. At this point things got serious real quick. I had one in elementary 1 in daycare and cared for the third child everywhere I went. Lord knows I was drowning and didn't know how to express my feelings to anyone. At times things got so tough I only had enough food to feed my children and not myself. #YOUDON'TKNOWMYSTORY...

As I reflect back, I also remember crying myself to sleep at night wondering how we were going to make it through the next day. Let me be honest, my pride had it through the next day. Let me be honest, my pride had set in so high that I hid a lot of things from my family and friends who really loved me and my children the most. Between both jobs and receiving some help from the government it still wasn't enough. I prayed and I cried, oh Lord just get us out of the situation.

The enemy had me thinking that i was only good for producing children and working two jobs that didn't equal up to #1. Having the responsibility of taking care of myself and others was a job all in itself. I got used to putting myself on the back burner, until that's what I did best. I didn't allow anyone or anything to come before my children. My parents taught me at an early age what's done in the dark comes to light so make it right.

#YOUDON'T KNOWMYSTORY...

As I approach the age of 26 I'm now carrying my fourth child. All I remember is going to my OBGYN to receive my new birth control, 15 minutes later the nurse comes back out and says. Ms O'Neal we can't help you with that today. Please make an appointment at the front and come back next month for your ultrasound. My heart dropped. I began to cry on Lord not me, thinking I was doing everything to protect myself from this happening again. My third child was finally going to the first grade and I was supposed to be home free. Depression kicked in so hard I was in denial for at least three months, how am denial for at least three months, how am I going to provide for another person.

When I tell y'all having my own relationship with God allow me to fight plenty of battles in my secret closet that no one ever knew about. I was actually feeling my bad days we're greater than my good ones. As time progressed I accepted the fact that God wouldn't put more on me than I could bear. I didn't know what the future entailed but one thing for sure I wasn't giving up. My children needed me more than I could ever imagine. #YOUDONTKNOWMYSTORY....

Having my own residence and a piece of car gave me some Independence to better our situation. I was able to work in between two particular daycares to lower my own child expenses, that lightened the load some. By this time my oldest was in Middle School and the other two were attending Elementary, my baby was in Pampers. Keep in mind I worked with children all day and still had to come home to be mama to my own. From helping with homework cooking, making bottles it seemed like I never had a break. After getting everyone showered and settled in bed, packing book bags at the front door for the next day became so habit forming it made me into the person I am today.

I'm very cautious about time and making sure things are right in place. Being a single parent at a early age, are right in place. Being a single parent at an early age, taught me how to become an adult really fast. I had to make plenty of decisions even if I was uncertain if they were right or wrong. It's clear to say that my children and I grew up together. I was responsible for taking care of someone other than myself at 17. I seriously don't think that my children ever knew that we were poor. They didn't wear everything by name brand, but trust and believe they were always clean. I kept the boys haircut and my daughter look like a princess at all times #YOUDONTKNOWMYSTORY...

My children were a reflection of me even if I had to wear the same thing over. I made sure they never had to. Finding a clothing store that offered layaway became my best friend. Twice a month I was able to pay off one and start all over again. During this time I had a full-time job working at the hospital and part-time making minimum wages working at an athletic shoe store just to make ends meet. I finally felt like I was able to inhale and exhale. The road I have traveled hasn't been easy, but God Made A Way.

Let me Fast Forward into my children's teen years. During this time I had 3 + High School one attending middle. My oldest son started his first job working at Subway inside of a gas station. Things were still a little difficult for us, having to work two jobs also making sure their everyday activities were still in place. The more they grew the bigger the bills became. Our

The more they grew the bigger the bills became. Our only reliable car broke down, immediately things began to take a turn for the worst. I had to quit my part time job, because I didn't want to rely on others to take me back and forth. Remember what I said earlier being prideful could hurt you. #YOUDONTKNOWMYSTORY...

By this time my oldest son started feeling himself hanging out with the wrong crowd, got into some trouble and went to jail. Lord knows that's all I need to hear. I immediately began to blame myself, because of the bad decision he chose to make. I felt if so my world just turned upside down, oh God how are we going to get past this. I gave them all my love and affection, so why is this happening to me. I clearly remember that day as if it was yesterday. The principal called your son was just arrested and had drugs in his position. I remember shouting from the top of my lungs oh no not my son. This is a "Mother's" worst nightmare.

From one gut punch to another, it felt like things were spinning out of control. I wasn't going to church frequently and felt God wasn't listening to my prayers. During this particular time my middle son wanted to play football and of course he had to have an athletic physical. One simple appointment turned into, EKG stress test Echo Etc. Things begin to get serious real fast. I test Echo Etc. Things begin to get serious real fast. I immediately began to pray Please Lord don't punish my children because of my wrongdoing. As my 16 year old son and I wait in the examination room I begin to cry, not knowing what to expect next. The doctor into the room and said he's going to need "OPEN HEART" surgery soon as possible #BUTGOD....

Lord I Need You Right Now!!!!!!! I'm a firm believer that God will use certain things and situations to gain your attention. I went from dealing with my oldest son concerning the police and now this. WHY IS THIS HAPPENING!!! I'm not embarrassed or ashamed to say I begin to question God on his actions. This led me to having a conversation with him daily, again he knows how to seek your attention. Me being weak at this point crying and praying that's all I knew how to do. #YOUDONTKNOWMYSTORY...

I learned real quick that Faith wasn't about asking God to stop the storm it was trusting him to help you through it. I begin to change a lot of things starting with myself. From getting on my knees praying and turning down my plate too fast. This issue we were facing was bigger than us. The next day I hit the reset button and truly let go of my pain hurt or anything else that may be hindering my inner peace.

That following week I gathered my children up and we headed down to MUSC in Charleston. In spite of me praying and fasting, the anxiety I was feeling driving miles away was unexplainable, and I really didn't know what to expect throughout this whole situation. Meanwhile the kids were playing in the backseat, and I was crying on the inside. A small voice quickly reminded me that he had this. My son's surgery was very successful, only because of God's Grace and Mercy. #YOUDONTKNOWMYSTORY...

We made it back home safely and things we're looking good for a while. Two years later I am running around trying to take care of loose ends to get my daughter preparing for graduation. All I was looking forward to is one more down and two more to go. Boy oh boy, I got hit with the unthinkable. I found out my daughter was 4 weeks pregnant before her graduation. This brought back so much pain and hurt, me not wanting her to experience the same embarrassment that I went through. Here I go again questioning God "Why". She was supposed to break the generational curse. I was thinking this is a test to see if I would lose faith. #YOUDONTKNOWMYSTORY...

My parents supported me and I was going to do the same by her. Things were a little rough around the edges at first, but we made it through our ups and down. My daughter definitely was paying attention down. My daughter definitely was paying attention to the struggle. This young lady had the mindset regardless of what I'm going to take care of what I produce. Remember it's not so much of what you say to your children, it's your actions that they respond to. My daughter worked a part-time and full-time job throughout her entire pregnancy. She told me no matter what they would be straight. Her grind was so real, it was scary sometimes. It felt like I was looking in the mirror at myself. She was blessed to provide a place of her own before her daughter turned too. They're doing well and still live in the state of South Carolina.

The single parent struggle isn't over yet It hurts when you go through something that kills you inside and you continue to walk around as if it's not affecting you at all. Money was still funny and the bills were frequently rolling. Around this time the older three were gone, my youngest and I reside in a three bedroom house that was running me $980 a month. Me using every outlet that I had no child support, still maintaining a car trying to buy grocery keep Shoes clothes on his back was difficult month to month. I remained humble as I could, didn't want him to see that I was failing by the wayside. This young man was so smart, I couldn't hide much from him. He still managed to keep a high grade point average even though things weren't going particularly well at home. #YOUDONTKNOWMYSTORY...

That prideful mind that I was caring for not only affected me but it took a toll over my children. My youngest knew we didn't have much, but he went alone as if we did. I barely could keep enough food in the house to provide for him and myself. Also trying to keep up an image I clearly couldn't afford. No matter what I did, it seems like it was never enough. It got so bad at times I even had to depend on my oldest son to pick up the broken pieces. Still not letting my family in knowing the level of stress I was under.

It was finally time for my youngest to graduate, and I really wanted him to attend college. In the midst of all of this the house that we were staying in went up for sale and I couldn't afford to purchase it. This all took place in the middle of his 12th grade year. We ended up moving out and had to reside with my daughter and her family for a while. I was feeling less than my title of being "Mom" #YOUDONTKNOWMYSTORY...

My son and I went from having our own privacy, until I was sleeping with my three-year-old granddaughter and he had to sleep between the couch and their living room floor. I felt suffocated and drowning all at the same time, again the only thing I knew was to work, hide the pain and keep it moving. Life has a way of throwing you curveballs and distractions just so you can lose your Faith.

As time went on my youngest decided to sign up for the military, because he knew I couldn't afford for him to attend college. He never shared this with me, but I felt he made this conscious decision so that we could have our own again. I eventually moved out of my daughters residence and got my own place again. My sense of Independence immediately kicked back in. #YOUDONTKNOWMYSTORY...

Things were moving so fast, my son went from boot camp AIT and deployed all in a year and a half. Before leaving the United States he was able to work extremely hard and purchase his first vehicle. At this point in my life I was so proud of my children, because they all had their own sense of independence.

Everyone was working including myself taking care of what we knew best "Family" I taught my children at an early age, to be there for one another no matter what the situation maybe. Things began to turn around in my favor, didn't know how to begin or where to even start. I always wanted to provide and help where there was a need in our less fortunate homeless community. #YOUDONTKNOWMYSTORY...

Speeding forward with my story. Me questioning my doubts and fears. How was I going to begin feeding the less fortunate when I was barely making ends meet for myself. I fell back and allowed God to lead the way. I'm now proud to announce that I am the CEO of my own non-profit organization called "Living In The Shadows" With the help of my #4 children #6 Grands family and friends, monthly we set out to feed over a hundred plus people twice a month. I also create different events, to meet the needs with socks, clothing Etc.

Having that strong love and support from my children/ grands, showed me that giving up was not an option. I Ms. Angelic O'Neal also has the title of being a Public Notary of Columbia South Carolina.

Before gaining the strength of telling you my naked truth. I had to Humble myself Fast and pray, go to God and ask him to give me the right words to say. God chose the path he desired for me to have. I'm very thankful and grateful for all that at the same time. I will continue to walk by faith and not by sight. My Best Is Yet To Come.

I will always remember sharing my naked truth as a single parent could save someone else's life.

#YOUDONTKNOWMYSTORY...

Note

Abuse

Let It Go!

By Chyvonne K.

"To carry a grudge is like being stung to death by one bee."

William H. Walton

I was sitting here thinking and reflecting on a major move I made in my life. I chose to LET IT GO. I could have continued to allow some things to interfere with my life and my efforts for upward mobility. Instead, I chose to release "IT." I simply said, *deje' van*! and I *let go* of the things that I had allowed to interrupt my life for too many years. "IT" was disturbing my peace of mind and oftentimes my daily activities, entangling and captivating my very present thoughts. I could not focus because I delved into fits of anger and resentment toward certain people in my life. I would see these people, speak to these people, think about these people, and immediately become disengaged with whatever I was doing or whomever I was communicating with.

I was stuck in a web of hurt from past situations, relationships, and circumstances. The short of it was, I was an emotional wreck!

"IT" had a hold on me like none other. I couldn't shake it or perhaps I didn't want to. Sadly, it seemed like every time I moved forward in my life and opened up to new people and new experiences, somehow, the old mind would find a way to creep back up. I would find myself stuck like a deer looking into the headlights of a hunter's truck in fear of moving one step further.

I was looking for "love," as so many people often say, in all the wrong places. What I was learning was that the sexual abuse I had encountered at the tender age of four years made me feel un-pretty, even at the age of 24. I was searching for admiration, acknowledgement, understanding, comfort, acceptance, and just plain "feel good." Dejectedly, no matter where I looked, I could not find any of those things. Or if I did, things would be really good for a while, and then the "source" of those wonderful "feelings" would begin to gradually fade away from me...and I again would seemingly be alone. I couldn't figure out how I kept ending up alone. Involved in random relationships and situationships, and still alone. Standing in a crowded room full of laughter, fun and friends; yet still alone. Hearing I love you from many, but not the one voice I wanted so much to hear, or the one heart I wanted to touch.

Then one day I had an epiphany. You know something like Oprah's AHA Moment! I had realized what the problem was. I had yet to deal with the "root" of my personal issues. Thus, I was seeking outward to create my internal happiness. I realized this was something that only I was responsible for, not other people or things. My own happiness was dependent upon how I allowed my surroundings, mishaps, and daily HAPPenings to affect my inner peace; negatively or positively. It was again back to MY CHOICE to either let go or hold on.

I believe T. Jefferson defined it best when he said, "happiness is not being pained in body or troubled in mind." I realized that I could control the pain in my body by dealing with the pain in my mind. I had clarity and I understood how I had never truly confronted the people who caused me so much pain in the first place. I had never fully dealt with the source of my pain.

All these years I was doing nothing but overriding the pain with newfound happiness, and newfound affection. I was fleeing to new places, I had more money, and a bunch of things. The bottom line though. I had never FORGIVEN them for hurting me, so in turn I could not LET IT GO.

Not many years ago, I confronted the "root" of my past pain and hurt, and I Let IT Go.

I forgave them for child sexual abuse. I forgave them for not listening to my innocent cry for help. I forgave them for not believing me. I forgave them for not knowing what to do to handle the situation. I forgave them for not being who and what I needed them to be...my savior. I took my power back. I closed a chapter in my life by choosing to save myself...I decided to choose peace.

I turned the page to continue on the journey I had begun and stopped so many times before. I realized that my life is like an open book, and I have the pen in my hand. I have the power to not necessarily change the situations, but I can choose how I am affected by the outcome and the final pages of whatever chapter I am in.

Claudia Black said, "Forgiving is not forgetting, it is remembering and letting go." I didn't in any way forget what happened or how I had felt as a child even into my adult years, but I made the conscious choice to "let it all go." Consequently, I remember not so I can dwell on the past or let it revive itself and reopen old wounds. Instead I remember because it allows me to see just how far I have come, and what I was strong enough to not only survive but conquer.

The past has now become a *stepping stone* for me to climb higher instead of a crutch, an excuse for me to keep walking with a limp. By letting go, I release the pain and ill feelings caused by such horrid memories, never to be re-lived.

I... have...PEACE...OF...MIND.

Today I walk in PEACE, I am FREE, I am comforted, I am admired, I am acknowledged, I am understood, I am accepted, and I am loved. Most importantly, I have learned what it means to take care of me and how to LOVE MY DARN SELF, even my flaws! I have no ill pain in the body, and I am no longer troubled in my mind. I understand who I am and that without pain there is no gain. I am learning how to be a better me every day. At times there is trial and error, yet I journey on. For the first time in a long time, I AM HAPPY. I AM ME and I AM OKAY.

TO ALL MY GIRLS OUT THERE, WHAT CAN I SAY, Dejé Van! LET "IT" GO! It's your CHOICE. Your happiness depends on YOU! I challenge you to walk in your own freedom and victory while declaring every day that #I'mPossible!

From The Sentiments of My Heart.

Note

From Broken 2 Freedom

By Ondia Wyatt Petty

Have you ever looked at a person and wondered why they act like they do? Especially when they seem to be a little unstable, whether it be emotionally, mentally, physically, and/or even sexually. Unstableness is a sign of some type of abuse. Allow me to walk you through a series of abuse in my life that eventually led me to becoming an abuser.

June 4, 1982 was the day my life officially began. Not knowing what was ahead but at that point I had no choice but go forth and live on. My mother gave birth to me in the Wake County Women's Institute in Raleigh, N.C. And of course she wasn't allowed to keep me, the warden called her family and said if no one comes to claim this child, she will be a ward of the state. My grandmother at the time was not thinking about raising another baby especially when all of her children were good and grown.

Luckily, I had a cousin that was willing and able to come pick me up. You would think that would have been the best decision for me but as I grew older there was a change of opinion.

See my cousin was older, had children of her own, she was saved, very active in the church, hardworking and dependable. Only thing lacking was she had lots of issues from her past that she never dealt with which caused her to lash out at us. Her trauma caused me and my cousins to experience physical/emotional abuse and bullying in the home. If one person got in trouble for the slightest thing, we all had to suffer the consequences. She would have us get naked, lay across the bed with our arms and legs stretched out while she beat us with a belt until she got tired. Sometimes it felt like she never got tired because it went on and on and on. There was not verbal abuse because I honestly cannot remember ever hearing her talk to me other than telling me, I'm about to beat you or go study whatever our scripture was we had to learn. And if we didn't know it, we had to stay up until it was learned or get beat. All of this started at the age of four or maybe five years old and ended in her household until I was about ten years old. Her behavior rubbed off on her son and he would bully me, picking on me, and playing with guns; telling me it's time for me to die by putting the gun to my head. He would pretend to pull the trigger and laugh. My cousin terrorized me so bad that I had to quote the scripture "For God has not given me the spirit of fear but a spirit of love, power, and a sound mind" every day and night because I was so afraid of everything. I watched my cousin who was very angry abuse her children, then turn around and abuse me (physical and emotional), which her toxicity spilled over on her children and they began to bully me (emotional and mental), which eventually spilled over on me.

Here I am now in the second grade and I'm frustrated and tired. Yes, a child my age was tired of this toxic life, living fearfully, and sore physically. So, I got to school one day and told the teacher I didn't want to go home, because I'm afraid of always having to go home and be alone for a while until someone gets home. I honestly didn't know what I was telling at the time, but by the time I got off the bus, and walked to the door, I was greeted with my bags packed and told I was being taken to my grandmother's house because social services was stepping in because of a report that was made. This was a relief. So, I thought.

I was placed with my grandmother and she wasn't saved, nor did she go to church. As a matter of fact, she had a bar in the back of her house, she smoked cigarettes faithfully, she was a part of the Elks Lodge and they partied regularly. I mean people were in and out. For a child my age, this was not what I needed to be around, but it didn't matter because I was with my grandmother and my heart was happy. My mother was still in prison, so I didn't talk to her or see her. Honestly, I never met her until I was nine years old.

My grandmother had a very different way of communicating with me once I moved in with her. It was almost like not communicating, if that makes sense. I would try to talk to her, and she would look at me with a look of disgust as if I had ruined her day, better yet, her life. So, I would back off because I felt like I was a problem. When she did need me or talk to me, she yelled at me constantly. That made me angry because I would have to watch her talk to other people and she would smile, laugh, and talk peacefully to them, but I got different at home. I never talked about it to anyone because well who did I have to talk to?

Eventually my grandmother gave her life to Christ and started going to church regularly, she became the president of the missionary board, the president of the kitchen committee and a deaconess. So once again we were at every church event and I was always the only child at some of the outreach programs. I was cool with it because I learned a lot and people got to know me. All of my family attended the same church and I loved it. I figured once my grandmother got saved her attitude towards me would change but it didn't. I just didn't understand what I did that made her hate me so much. But I guess if I were living my life child free for the longest then all of a sudden, I have to raise my granddaughter, I probably would be a little upset too.

The day came for me to finally meet my mother and several months before, she told me that I would be coming to live with her. I was excited and nervous at the same time because I didn't know her like that. In reality I was going to be moving in with a complete stranger. I told all my friends I wouldn't see them the next year and we all cried and had a going away party because my mom promised me, I'd be living with her. Meanwhile, my mother was released from prison and I met her. We didn't bond at all!! Something just didn't feel right. So later that night she called me in the room and told me I couldn't move in with her because her and her boyfriend didn't have the space, so I had to stay with my grandmother. All I could say was okay, but my heart was bleeding. I had never had my hopes up that high and then let down. I got over it as time progressed and she was in and out of my life. She would bring gifts by to pacify me, but I longed for a mother daughter relationship. She asked me one day what was one thing that I really wanted to do, and I told her I wanted to go skating. We attempted to go skating maybe four times and it was not a success either time. My mom had a habit of lying to me and coming to pick me up saying we were going to do one thing but doing another. She would use me to go hang out with other men and their children. She would lay up with the men and I would have to play with the children. But yet, all I wanted was a relationship with my mother. I had questions about life that only a mother could answer. She just wasn't available!

The last day we attempted to go skating is a day I'll never forget. My mom was drunk and she picked me up. So now we're on the way to the skating rink and she drives around the curve and swerves. Next thing you know we get pulled over, but guess what? We were three minutes from the skating rink. Long story short my mom goes to jail and I got her things and the police took me home to my grandmother. I called my mom's boyfriend to let him know and he decides he wants to talk a little. We talked! He asked questions and I answered. I volunteered information, not really knowing what was about to happen. He went to get my mom out of jail, and she comes straight to the house to get her things but comes in upset. Now this whole time my grandmother hasn't come in to ask me am I okay, but she sees the sadness and worry on my face but neglects to discuss anything. Moving on, my mom storms in my room and yells "why did you take my purse out of the car? You should have just left everything and the next time you want to tell something you need to think twice, so from here on out don't call me because I don't want to talk to you anymore. I'm not playing, don't call me for nothing." Ma'am, I'm 12 years old and your child, how do you say things like that to someone you birthed and say you love? I forgot that all this time I had been around my mom, I never heard her say "I love you", she never hugged me or anything. It was always yelling, rejection, negligence, and putting everyone/everything else before me. I can remember the time being about 8:20pm and when she left the house, I felt like the scum of the earth. Everything I had been through had been bottled up and the time I finally opened up to talk about it, it backfired on me. Back in my shell I go.

Six months later, my mother still wasn't talking to me. There were days I would try to call her, and she wouldn't answer me, or I would dial the number but wouldn't press send. Christmas morning, around 7:12 am I heard the telephone ring and my grandmother answered. I opened my eyes and said to myself "My mom is dead!" My grandmother yelled my name and was crying and said exactly what I just said when I opened my eyes. My mom had died from a methadone overdose. She was with some guys and they were doing drugs, she overdosed, and they tried to put her in cold water to bring her back, but it was too late. So, they dropped her off at the emergency room exit at CMC hospital. Twelve years old and losing a parent that just told you not to ever talk to them again was rough, but I had to be strong for my grandmother and other family members. I suppressed all of my feelings and kept it moving.

After the funeral and burial, I returned to school and my attitude changed. I became very angry. It's like all I could think about was the abuse and trauma I had been through, so I lashed out at others. My mom had a child six months before she died, and he was in foster care for years, but he would come visit us for the weekend. I had so much anger built up that I would be mean to him just because I could. I started bullying people that I felt more superior than but on the flip side I was being bullied by children that intimidated me. How in the world does that work? I even pushed my grandmother and fought one of my Aunts and one of my Uncles. I mean I fought them like I was an adult. All the abuse and built up anger caused me to retaliate the way I did. My grandmother tried to get me to see a psychologist, but I was so stubborn and rebellious that I would not talk at the appointments. One thing I know is that if a person is not ready to receive help, going to counseling will be pointless.

My behavior was getting worse and I was getting out of control, almost unable to contain it. There was a lady that said God spoke to her and told her to adopt me and my grandmother agreed because she couldn't handle me. I knew the lady and her child, so I was comfortable moving in with them and I did. She was a little strict, but it was for a good cause. You can't get into college with bad grades, so we had to work hard to maintain a B. One day she came downstairs and said, "I didn't know you had breathing problems when you sleep." I responded, "I didn't either lol but how did you know?" She replied, "Oh I come in and lay with you every other night!" She was laughing and I looked at her like, why are you laughing? So she voluntarily says, "I like laying behind you and holding you." I knew she liked women because that was the lifestyle she lived, and I saw several women she was with. I felt like the laying with me was a bit weird and I desired a mother daughter relationship but not like that. Let's just say I didn't live with her long. I went through some sexual abuse from the lady and verbal abuse from her daughter that I was not able to handle. And of course I wasn't able to talk about it at the time, but I ended up getting suspended from school and was told I was giving their family a bad name, so I returned to my grandmother's house. Thank you Jesus!

Little did I know my grandmother was sick, so we had to move to another house. By this time my grandmother was on oxygen and had spent several months in the hospital on life support. I had to grow up fast and get a job so I could help my grandmother. I met some people around this time, and we hung out one night and had some drinks. No, I was not twenty-one yet, but I was intoxicated and there was a girl present that took advantage of me. I know you are wondering, how can a woman rape another woman, but it can happen. She penetrated me with her fingers, and she had long nails, so she was chopping up my cervix and blood was gushing from my vaginal area. When she was done, she left me there, and I eventually woke up and got myself together and went home. My grandmother was in the kitchen when I walked in the door but as usual, we didn't talk about anything. I went to shower and was extremely sore. I prayed to God because I felt horrible and it seemed like I was being punished for something. I couldn't understand why I was going through the crap I was going through. I mean God, do you really love me? After this situation happened, I was raped again, twice to be exact and these were by men. My mind was all messed up. I didn't want to be penetrated, I was still longing for a mother daughter relationship, I lacked affection, everyone I got close to died, I was lonely, and I was confused about if I wanted to be with a man or a woman. I loved the Lord, but I had experienced so much abuse in church that I wanted to stay away from church people. On top of that, because of the sexual abuse and the trauma caused from this, the doctors confirmed I would never be able to have children. My life sucks and I haven't even graduated high school yet.

My junior year, February 9, 1999 my grandmother transitioned about an hour after I left the hospital. That was the day I had cried and apologized, and I understood how sick she really was. Reality had set in and I had to accept and let her go. Once again, I had to be strong for everyone else when I had all these issues built up on the inside. I was left all alone because there was no one to help raise me. I was on my own at sixteen years old. There were people that offered their homes to me but of course there was a cost to pay. No one will do anything for free, but I paid what I had to and once I graduated high school I moved into my own apartment.

I went through my childhood life story to show how the things we go through as children affect us as adults. Mental, emotional, physical, sexual, and verbal abuse are toxic traits that transfer to others. If you do not deal with the root problem, then you will continue to be haunted by the problem. I experienced and encountered all of this abuse and never got the help I needed. I only suppressed my issues allowing them to stack on top of each other. This is not healthy. I eventually became my cousin, mother and grandmother to my children and others. I verbally, mentally, emotionally, and physically abused my children. Not purposely though. See, I never paid attention to the signs I displayed. Instead of talking to my babies, I yelled. I would call them names all because I was feeling down and depressed. The only way I knew to release it was through abuse. See had I been taught proper communication, proper ways to deal with anger, grief counseling, and if my guardians had been more patient with me; meaning taking me to counseling when I was ready; I believe I could have avoided the toxic spill over onto my children.

It wasn't until I matured in Christ, developed a real prayer life, allowed God to show me who I was versus who he wanted me to be, and allowed me to lose some people and things, that I was able to change the way I handled my children. I had to forgive myself for the things I did as a child and adult, so I was accountable for my own actions. I forgave my offenders even if they did not apologize to me. I acknowledged the pain and hurt which allowed me to release it and lay it at the altar. I let it go and did not turn back. I made a decision to be happy, healed, and whole. I knew that God had so much in store for me so I could no longer let the abuse and neglect of my past keep me bound from purpose. Find a counselor, therapist, or Certified Life Coach to talk to and never allow anyone or anything to hold you hostage in a place of abuse. Take authority and release yourself from bondage. I allowed God to take me from broken to FREEDOM by making a conscious decision to be better!

Note

Single Ladies

The Rescue From Within

By: Tonya Lewis-Rose
Manuscript

Hindsight is always 20/20 vision. I used to hear older people say that to me so many times. But as I grew, I began to learn the true essence of what that really meant. In my own words, that means that what was really visible all long I now see so much clearer. Then, it brings me to question what prompts such clarity of sight and mind? I have an answer for that. The things we suffer have a way of bringing us understanding that we normally do not get. Looking back over life there are so many things I wish I knew. So many missed opportunities that I wish I had taken advantage of and so many doors that I wish I possessed the wisdom to walk through. I would like to offer these few words of encouragement to you as you journey. Life does not come with a label. There is no blueprint outline that shows how to have a successful life or how to live a happy life.

Life is created by our combination of choices. Those choices that cultivate the type of life we live are good and bad choices. Good choices of course mostly yield good results. For instance, the more you read the more you want to read. For most we would say that's a good choice. Bad choices for the majority of us, are those choices that happen as a byproduct of us trying to pursue the good choice but just not meeting the mark. I found out that we as people have many options. How we choose is going to define how we live. No one intentionally sets out to make a bad choice; it kind of "just happens". What bothers me most is the fact that in all our striving to make the best out of life, bad things must happen. It's those things that teach us right from wrong and give us understanding. However, it's those same things that we tend to battle with so much until we become stuck in them rather than use them as bridges to take us over. This perpetual cycle causes us to live life searching for things that were always present from the very beginning. Those things that were given to us instinctively and divinely at birth. Our innate ability to do right or wrong. Our desire for choices and chances in life are steered from our experiences. How you experience life will be reflected in your responses. In retrospective view the rescue is within. When we look for answers externally it's only a quick fix. But, because we are programmed to look to our environment, families, education, or significant others for answers to things that we can only provide the real answers to. We spend sometimes years searching for a conclusion. On a quest for something that was never lost. Something that resides inside and is fully awake. Although, you might be asleep, the rescuer that lives in you never sleeps. It's that small still voice that speaks to you. Telling you what direction to take when you're in your most trying times of life. That nudge to go right when you desire to go left. That's the rescue! When we are unfamiliar with how he speaks and directs us we create casualties. Especially in the younger years of life. Better known as the tender years of life. The years when it doesn't take much to soften us. When we are not as affected by the cares of the world or blocked by the trials and tribulations that come to block our pathway. Those are the years that we should press the hardest. That's the prime time to maximize our momentum in life. So, in an effort to prevent the expansion and manifestation of our hopes, our dreams and passion, we self-sabotage with thoughts of lack. You know, those conversations in your head that say " you're not good enough" "you'll never be able to do that" "no one will ever love you like that" you're not pretty enough for him/her" or " you have nothing to offer them". These thoughts come to antagonize our thought process and evict our passion of pursuit. But knowing is half the battle. When we become fully aware of what we possess. it then becomes a weapon of defense versus a weapon of self-destruction. That's why we find it so trying to even educate ourselves on ways to be unstuck. I bet it took a lot for you to even come here today. So, I celebrate your decision to come. It's the best you could ever make. I want to reintroduce you to the rescue you have within you. No longer do you have to search for someone to save you. Look for love in places that are only able to give you love from a deficit. Perpetually searching from arm to arm for security that you were born with. Looking for peace in a place that was founded by chaos. All along crying out to be saved when the rescue is with you but because you can't identify who it is. You live life underprivileged.

The invisible scars are so much worse than the visible ones. It's imperative that we heal the invisible scars so we can heal our lives. Healing the places that we bleed on because of the wound not being properly treated. The wound of abandonment, mistrust and failures. These scars come and they take over the mind. They consume your thoughts and ultimately your actions. When we become acquainted with who the rescuer is in our life learn how to just BE. We learn it's ok not to give much thought to those things we see as beyond our control. We become aware that while it's great to have goals and plans for our life. There is always more than one path to achieve them. We tap into power to be BOLD. Instead of the belief of "I can't" being a self-fulfilling prophecy you get the strength and power to say I can do all things! I wish that I knew the power of being aware of what was inside of me. How to set the table. Setting the table is not about putting a place mat out for a friend at dinner. Setting the table means to make room for God. To create a space for him that you can hear him in. It's a placemat of awareness. A seat of investment. Because it's his desire that we be blessed. It's the will of the father to give us the kingdom. Yes, the enemy knows that if you ever become fully aware of what's in you then and only then will you tap into resources to give you victory. So he keeps you in self-pity about what you did not do. Questioning, the what ifs of life. What if I had done this or that differently? Would my marriage have survived? If I just listened to my parents more often. Would I not have had to experience being a teenage mother or father? Or here's the best one. If I was only born into another family. Maybe, I wouldn't have turned out like this. What brings you the most fear is what will set you free! Please understand that there is nothing that you can do that will change the plan and purpose of God in your life. Who you are is who he knew you would be even from your mother's womb? He has created you and made you as a vessel to bring him glory in the earth. Although, we look ourselves in the mirror and see this flawed image. God looks and sees an image of himself. Even in our most imperfect state God calls us beautiful. He provides a rescue for us. We don't have to search to find it because it's with us always. He understood our loud but oh so silent cries for help. When no one else understood. When others judged you at an opportunity that they could've helped.

God placed a rescue down inside that would speak to you in the midst of your tears. The rescue says fight harder, you can do this, brush yourself off and get back up, yeah you messed up, but you can get up. The rescue says that you are worthy and you are enough! All that you have to do in this process is agree. Often as we search for a rescue, we get so lost in the feeling that we can never bounce back from this or that we will never be able to be restored. I need to let you know that the restorer is with you! There is a comeback that is being birthed out of you. Out of that situation that brought you pain is a beauty that will bring you joy! To be rescued means to be delivered from a threat of destruction or defeat. To be removed from harm's way. When we really believe that he is with us our language changes. Our posture and approach to life's difficulties becomes so different. He steps in and makes the difference. Please notice I never said it would be easy, but he said he would be with you. We can then be honest and say, it hurts, I don't understand, I feel isolated and alone but I am going to go. He wants the real us! It's okay to be truthful because at that point he can then work through truth to bring you to a place of deliverance. He doesn't need us to be strong. Even though that's all we ever hear. Be strong, hold your head up, it's going to happen for you. God does not need your strength. He is strong. He is saying let me have all that pain and sorrow, all those tears. I will bottle them up and give you a brand-new hope and future. You must learn to accept the unconditional love that you deserve first to yourself and then to others. Once that's done be eager to give it tenfold in return. Have you ever looked at yourself in the mirror for a long period of time and just questioned how you got to where you are today? I mean uninterrupted just meditating on your life. I have and there were so many unanswered questions that I had to contend with. Questions of why I felt like it was never enough, why was I chosen for this path, who would do something like this to someone like me and God do you even hear me at all? The frustration of not knowing the answers caused years of sickness, unhappiness and mistrust. But one day while mirroring my life in a brand new perspective I learned that surely he had to be with me. Who else would heal me when the Doctors didn't understand my survival? When they expected that I should live life in partiality of the benefits as a kingdom citizen. But yet here I am with full access and dominion in the kingdom. I learned that the key to it all. See we live this life playing the game, but we don't play to win. Winning seems so far from achievement when we look at our current states. Dealing with so much from promiscuity, adultery, fornications, soul ties, low self-esteem, and abuse. It's easy to be lost in the transition of it all. I had to remind myself that he is a restorer. He will restore what the cankerworm and locust worm have eaten up. When I think about these kinds of worms, they are all metamorphic and they all came to pass. They came to produce a change in life. I am sure in the span of their life they couldn't imagine what life would be like after their current state, like many of us. They squirm around on their bellies just trying to survive. They become a touch point for the people.

But when God goes ahead of you he makes a way for change. He sends the rescue to introduce them to the butterfly that's lying asleep inside of the worm. God has already created us. He is all knowing and his grace is sufficient for us. We must not allow our environments to dilute our purpose.

So here the rescue comes to make a way for us. To deliver us not from others but mostly from ourselves. Before we can be anything to anyone, we must be what we need to ourselves. You must learn to invest in yourself. Only invest in others that are willing to invest themselves in you. Life is about the exchange. Too often we live giving more than we get in return. People that are toxic "takers" will always suck dry your energy and strength. Life has a way of persecuting you. Persecutions show up in so many ways. That husband or wife that walked out on you. Throwing away the love you wholeheartedly served them with. That young teenager who was shamed for having a baby out of wedlock, that couple who fought endlessly before their children, ultimately failing to show the love of God. However, none of this ever killed the plan for our lives. It only changed the position in which God will operate to rescue us. So if you have to cry at night, you will wake up in the morning and put on your full face and pursue the plan. You must know that the rescue is within. There is a king in you that wants to expand your view. He wants to show you how all those things that hurt you only were intended to help you. Your perspective must change. A perspective change is one that happens inwardly before anyone can ever see it outwardly. It's the invisible work of God that unlocks and destroys strongholds in our lives. It's the birthing of serious passion for what you're doing. The power to create! Speaking to my younger self I would say. Girl, don't worry, you got this. Yes, it's a setback but from a perspective view. It's just a setup. You don't have to look for anyone or anything to rescue you. Tap into the rescuer that is living inside you. You have got to believe that he wants to use you. He has a plan for your life. There is no place that you can go that will violate the plan he has for you. This opposition cannot discredit your ability. This is merely a force to raise you to the next dimension. Therefore, wipe your eyes and put on your best rags. There is a battle to fight and you have been equipped to fight it. Don't be consumed about the battle because the rescue is always in position to deliver you. He is in place to pull you when you go left and to correct you when you are wrong. You are in good company, no reason to worry or fear! Breathe everything will happen the way it's supposed to. Trust that he is with you no matter where you go. May the rescue of God find you in all things and teach you of his ways. Bringing you peace in every area of and in the process!

Note

Mental Health

Mental Health Awareness for Women

By Terronda L. Jackson

Mental Health should be a part of your routine, just like a yearly physical exam, pap smear, mammogram, etc., but often it goes ignored and pushed to the back burner. Women are notorious for caring for the needs of others and setting themselves aside for children, husband, aging parents, work, business, ministry, and school, etc. It's always one thing or another that prevents us from attending to our own psychological needs. Included in the next few paragraphs will be tips and pointers to stay on top of your mental game!

RECOGNIZING DEPRESSION – We have all experienced depression at some point in our lives. We have suffered losses and went through tough times in life. During those times it's normal to feel a bit down and maybe experience some depressive symptoms. Chronic depression can surface as emotional, spiritual, and physical symptoms.

- Emotionally, depression may manifest as worry, shame, sadness, nervousness, and even fear. Some even have trouble concentrating and find that the things that once brought them joy don't anymore. Everything may seem hard and one can't seem to get through the most menial tasks.
- Spiritually, you may struggle with feelings of loss of purpose and meaning to life. You may feel unbalanced, numb, or even disconnected from family, friends, and career. You just want to be left alone.
- Physically, depression can surface as feelings of lack of motivation or energy, restlessness, and lack of follow-through.

RECOGNIZING ANXIETY – Experiencing anxiety is a normal part of everyday life. If you get a new job or have to take a test you may experience anxiety. However, the presence of unbearable anxiety all day every day on a daily basis is not normal, it can and will wear you down. Chronic anxiety leaves you feeling:

- Worn out and tired on most days, both mentally and physically
- Can last for weeks, months, even years with fluctuating intensity depending on what life cycle you are in
- Physically, anxiety can manifest itself as chest pains, flashes of cold and heat, breathing problems, increased heart rate, racing and unsettled thoughts

BRIEF DESCRIPTIONS OF THREE TYPES OF ANXIETY

Generalized Anxiety Disorder – Generalized Anxiety Disorder is the most commonly diagnosed form of anxiety. It is when a person worries about more than one thing all the time, not just one specific thing. It usually affects women more so than men. It can be hard to control because it's not specific to any one thing, but encompasses one's entire life and everything in it.

Obsessive Compulsive Disorder – Obsessive Compulsive Disorder is a condition which includes unwanted, persistent, and intrusive thoughts, ideas, or the compulsion to perform repetitive actions over and over.

Phobias – A condition in which an individual will go to great lengths to avoid a particular person, place, or thing as to avoid experiencing the extreme irrational fear associated with "it". This condition can be as extreme to leave an individual unable to leave their home for anything at all.

Panic Disorder – Symptoms include sweating, rapid breathing, chest pains, loss of control, and fear. Panic attacks can be very intense and can occur and escalate very quickly, but could take some time to go away. Individuals feel real and genuine danger despite there being no signs of imminent danger around.

PTSD or Post Traumatic Stress Disorder – could be the result of being involved in a highly stressful event that was outside of one's control, such as war, rape, domestic abuse, gun violence, physical assault, or natural disaster such as a hurricane, flooding, etc. Symptoms include avoidance, flashbacks, nightmares, and anxiety

DECREASING STRESS – While stress can be a healthy motivator at times, too much stress can be harmful; therefore, it is important to keep our stress levels low.

- Learn who and what stresses you the most. It is important to be able to identify triggers associated with the onset of episodes of stress.
- Learn when and where you are more prone to be stressed. Identify certain places and certain times of the year that may cause you to be more emotionally sensitive. Be aware of anniversaries of stressful events such as death, divorce, and other loss.
- Do not hold grudges or stay angry for long periods of time. Forgive and let go quickly. Forgiveness is for you and your well-being. You may hold a grudge, while the other party has gone on living their best life. Let it go.
- Learn when stress is affecting you in a negative manner. Never allow anyone to take you out of character. Recognize stress and call it what it is.

PHYSICAL HEALTH – Good physical health is also important in maintaining good mental health.

- Develop an exercise routine working your way up from 2 days a week to at least 3-4 days per week.
- Eat healthy balanced meals with adequate portions
- Stay hydrated, drink 6-8 glasses of water each day to replenish and flush toxins from the body
- Get adequate sleep each night, depending on your

activity level, between 7-9 hours of rest is needed to allow our body to repair and regenerate healthy cells. It also allows our minds ample time to rest and process information from each day.

LEARN TO RELAX – Learning to take small relaxation periods throughout your day can be a total game changer. Even if it's just for a few minutes, JUST DO IT!

- On the ride to and from work turn the radio off. Learn to enjoy you in solitude. Be present in the moment with yourself. If you must have music listen to relaxing sounds like jazz or instrumental versions of music you enjoy.
- If you feel tense or tired at work take a 2-3 minute bathroom break, get up, walk around your office or even outside to get fresh air if you can. Tense muscles in the upper body, head, shoulders, and neck may cause you to be more prone to headaches.
- Don't get so worked up about things you can't change. Remember, it is what it is and you cannot control it. You are only in control of you.
- Limit arguments and disagreements. You are not always going to get along with everyone, sometimes you have to "agree to disagree", and that's OK. Your peace is important.

What I'm trying to say is, "Ladies please take care of yourself, there's only one you." When you go to the doctor for your yearly checkup please have a conversation about your current state of mind. Don't be afraid to have the conversation about feelings, thoughts, and emotions. The days are long gone when women were expected to stay barefoot, pregnant, and at home. The truth is we lead full lives outside of the home to include full-time careers, businesses, and then we happily return home in the evening to work full-time and serve our families. All I ask is that we do it from a mentally healthy place!!!

Terronda L. Jackson, MA, NCC, LPC

Note

Disclaimer

This Content is not intended to be a substitute for professional medical advice, diagnosis, or treatment. Always seek the advice of your physician or other qualified health provider with any questions you may have regarding a medical condition.

Directory of Authors

Ondia Wyatt Petty, Clc, LPN
From Broken To Freedom Life Coaching and Mentoring services, LLC
Email: Ondia.pettylifecoach@yahoo.com
Telephone number: (704) 477-5697

Tonya Rose
Email:EldTRoseMinisters@gmail.com
Telephone:(803) 470-6726

Raynotta Marrie Brooks BA
Email: RayRaymtay@aol.com

Terronda L. Jackson MA, NCC, LPC
True Light Counseling and Consulting LLC
Website: truelightcounseling.wixsite.com
Telephone: (803) 265-5515

Constance Purnell LPC
Constance7purnell@gmail.com
(803) 724-8245

Ig: constance_the_legendary
Fb: Constance Purnell
Website: constanthelegendary.as.me

Elise Reid
My Go 2 LLC
Email: Terragilmore@mygo2ll.com
Website: www.Mygo2llc.com

Chyvonne Kimbrough MBA,MLS
I'mPossible Life Coaching
Email: ClKimbrough8@gmail.com
Website: Im-possiblelifecoach.com

Angelic O'Neal
Living in the shadows Non Profit LLC
(803) 357-5930

Taisha' O'Neal BA, Clc, LPC
Website: www.Taishanichole.com
Taisha@taishanichole.com
(202)838-7429

Made in the USA
Columbia, SC
13 July 2020

13782848R00093